# Once A Poem A Time

## The Life and Memory of Amare Burruss

IM Creation (P.Thompson)

BookLeaf Publishing

India | USA | UK

Made with ❤ on the BookLeaf Publishing Platform
www.bookleafpub.in
www.bookleafpub.com

# Dedication

To the loving memory of my first born grandson **Amare Burruss June 17,2004 - December 7, 2022.** He would have been so vocally, proud of and excited for me for moving forward with my dream.

# Preface

In the pages of this book you will find my heart as a living breathing testament to the life and memory of Amare Burruss. Having someone you love murdered is like having someone reach inside your heart and rip it out completely.  After his life was taken away from us in 2022, I knew that I had to experience my life differently.  I pray that as you read these poems about Amare that you will come to understand him and what he means to me. As I walk through this journey, I realize that I had to change my reaction to the things of the world and writing this poetry book is about learning how to do that.

# Acknowledgements

I want to Acknowledge all of the following people who
are my love, joy and happiness.


My Niece

**Nell** who has stayed by our side, supported us with
love,friendship, hope and endurance. who taught me
how to love and it is because of you that I understand
dedication and devotion.


My Darling Daughters

**Asia and Erica** thank you for being the best things that
have ever happened to me. The joy and love that I have
garnered throughout my life with you is only surpassed
by the love you have shown me. I hope and pray that I've
been the mother you needed to be the best person you
could become.


My Beautiful Granddaughters

**Aniyra** you have become such an awesome and excellent
young women. Watching you grow into who you are and
have always been "a major force " to reckon with in this
world, has given me immeasurable joy. I pray that you
will continue to grow and flourish all the day of your

life.


**Aerishaya** you have such a beautiful mind and strong athletic body that you are able to make yield to you will. Continue to hone your skill don't forget to seek out areas to grown in and where you can become exceptionally you in your chosen sport and continue to challenge you only against you. Never compete with anyone else. Your talents are uniquely yours


My Handsome Grandsons
**Asaru** it has been an amazing journey with you watching you grow into a young man that makes his family proud. You are a leader and a quiet protector of your siblings and strength of your family.


**Akiel** you are such a talent in your own right although you are the youngest you have made a unique place for yourself in your family. You have a phenomenal mind, physical skill and dazzling charm that will allow you to chose your own path. Whatever you choose believe in yourself and you will succeed.


To my family both big or small, no matter what I love you all. I'm sorry to some, because I couldn't be who you needed to be, but know in my heart I love you all unconditionally.

# 1. Amare's Birthday June 17, 2002

On that 17th night in June, before he was born things got
very scary.
They rushed her to a room, and her eyes got very teary.

The room they put her in was brightly lit
I stood outside that room scared and trying not to throw
a fit.

The nurse called me "mom" and said "We need her to
relax.
We're doing all we can to keep her still, but she keeps
fighting us back."

The anesthesiologist said, "We need to put her to sleep
and we don't have long.
Is there something you do?" and I started singing her a
song.

He held the mask on her face, and I sang as she finally

went to sleep.
I held my hand on her head and prayed, "Dear Lord, her
soul to keep."

They did a c-section to get him out and finally he was
free,
from the cord that was around his neck, and she named
him Amare'.

# 2. The Weeks that Followed

Later that week the doctor said she was well enough to
take Amare' home.
From that moment on it was her and him. She was happy
and never moaned or groaned.

Those first days for her were full of wonder and surprise
He grew so fast that she couldn't believe her eyes.

Everyone who met Amare' fell in love with him.
His big dark brown eyes and his big ole toothless grin.

Before she knew it he was learning how to talk
And at just nine months old he was learning how to
walk.

He was such a rough and tumble little boy.
He loved to play with trucks, cars and all kinds of toys.

One day at dinner, his mother called me and said,
"You won't believe it. This boy put the spaghetti and the

bowl on top of his head."

I remember the birthday parties she threw for him at two
and three,
What a wonderful child Amare' was growing to be.

We had some of the problems, the same kind other
parents had raising kids,
A too playful boy, some sleepless nights and some
illness, yes we did.

He was strong-willed and bold, sometimes quiet and
sometimes loud
He was a little rambunctious, but his mother could
control him, so he wasn't too wild.

While he was still a baby, she went back to school to
finish what she hadn't completed at the start,
She said, "Cannot be a dumb mother and have a kid; no
that's not smart."

She wanted to be able to answer his questions knowing
he'd have quite a few.
Especially later when it was time for him to go to
school.

# 3. Day Care Stunner Amare'

I remember when Amare' was in daycare. When he
walked in, the kids would cheer.
They would get so excited to see him after he'd yell,
"Hello, I'm here."

If I hadn't seen it with for myself, I'd think somebody
was lying,
But I was shocked. I called his mom and was laughing so
hard I was crying.

This little fellow walked into the room and one little girl
started taking off his coat,
And another little girl was holding a lollipop while he
licked and yeah, I know, believe me, they were doing the
most.

# 4. Amare' Went to School to Learn

Amare' had a lot of friends and family who loved him.
He showed love and appreciation for each one of them.
One summer when his cousin from Connecticut came
down,
Amare' asked if he could go with them and spend the
summer out of town.
That's how his Connecticut summer got started.
Because his cousin's family was so open hearted.
He spent as many summers in Connecticut as he
possibly could.
They had him in different types of summer camps and
that for him was good.
His sister went to visit family in Delaware for her
summers of play.
I'd missed them every summer that they went away.
They missed each other, so much in fact,
You couldn't separate them when they got back.
They rode their bikes, played together in or outside,
They only had a few weeks to play before the first day of

school would arrive.

# 5. Summers in Connecticut

Amare' had a lot of friends and family who loved him.
He showed love and appreciation for each one of them.
One summer when his cousin from Connecticut came
down,
Amare' asked if he could go with them and spend the
summer out of town.
That's how his Connecticut summer got started.
Because his cousin's family was so open hearted.
He spent as many summers in Connecticut as he
possibly could.
They had him in different types of summer camps and
that for him was good.
His sister went to visit family in Delaware for her
summers of play.
I'd missed them every summer that they went away.
They missed each other, so much in fact,
You couldn't separate them when they got back.
They rode their bikes, played together in or outside,
They only had a few weeks to play before the first day of
school would arrive.

# 6. Winters at Home

The long cold winter days that ended with long warm
nights at home.
We enjoyed those warm nights together after school and
work even when we wanted some time alone.
As each one hurried in, we couldn't wait to greet one
another.
Amare' and his sister couldn't wait to run in to see their
mother.
Homework time could turn into a struggle, when Amare
didn't want to get it done,
While mom was trying to prepare a meal for us it wasn't
any fun.
We weren't the family whose kids had TVs, computers or
video games in their rooms.
They were set up where we could see them, because we
did not want to presume.
We were aware that there were predators all over the
internet.
We didn't want to be amiss in watching over them. We

didn't want them to do something that they might just regret.

The long cold winter days that ended with long warm nights at home.

We enjoyed those warm nights together after school and work even when we needed space to be alone.

We had movie nights, game nights, but story times were the best because everyone got to talk about what they wanted to share.

We talked about things that bothered us, and we listened to each other with care.

It wasn't all hearts and flowers. We had our troubles too.

We had hard times and bad times and lived in different homes.

Unfortunately there were quite a few unknowns.

We loved the long winter days and the long winter nights.

Sometimes we got cabin fever. We'd argue, but we'd never fight.

The adults would go to their corner, and you know what Amare' or his sister would do, They'd say something funny to break the ice and the next thing you know everyone was cool.

# 7. High School years

When Amare' was in high school, it seemed like he had
so much fun.  He had good and bad days. Sometimes
he'd get in trouble.
His mom had a village, and we helped her to raise her
son. Whenever we were needed, someone would show
up on the double.
"It wasn't me", he always had a reason as to why he
wasn't wrong.
He alway had a story to tell; it was like he was singing a
song.
"See, Ma-ma, let me explain what happened because it
wasn't my fault,"
But he wasn't good at lying with a straight face, so
eventually his lying came to a halt.
I went up to the school several times, and it was the
same ole' thing.
The teacher said that the boy won't shut his mouth.
That's what the teachers told my mom, he was like me I
had no doubt.

He did his homework sometimes and other times he did
not.
He'd give some kind of excuse or tell the teacher he
forgot.
I'd remind him about when he was younger, and he said
he wanted to go to school to learn.
He just looked at me silently, because he knew Ma-ma
was getting concerned.
His mother kept him looking good and that helped him
to feel great.
His clothes were nice, his hair stayed cut, and he had
what they call "sea sick" waves.

# 8. Summer Job Years

No more Connecticut summers. That young man had to
go to work.
He had to make his own money to pay for all his pants
and shirts.
Let's not talk about his tennis shoes; that man's feet
were dressed to kill
And every time he brought a pair out it would give the
people a thrill.
One day someone asked where did you get those shoes.
Amare' just simply told him you got to learn how to
make these moves.
Each year no matter where he worked for the summer
they all loved him - the staff, the clients and his peers.
It was almost like he was back in Day Care, when they
saw him they would  literally cheer.
He worked hard for two summers and was told that he'd
done great work.
They told me, "Your grandson has good manners. We

knew he had some neatness quirks.

# 9. The Basketball After School Day

Amare' loved to play basketball. He started playing ball
in middle school.
He focused on being good and wanted to win if he
could.
In those days he wasn't very tall and the guys he played
with weren't a joke in size at all.
I remember one day when I came to pick him up, they
were picking him up off the floor.
I was angry when that giant coach fell on him just as I
walked through the door.
I ran over to check on him, and the coach was so
apologetic.
He said somehow I lost my balance and he was behind
me. I was mad, but I guess I did get it.
We got him up. He said he wasn't hurt and that he said
he was okay.
The coach and I were worried,so we took him to see the
doctor anyway.
The doctor checked him out and said his foot was

sprained, he had not broken a bone. Amare asked, "Am I okay to play?" The coach said no, you're going home. Amare' asked if he could still play. Mom said "in about two weeks you can be back on the court."
That little boy was so restless, Man, how he loved that sport.

# 10. Going to Texas in the Pandemic

In 2021 we went to visit our family who lived in Texas.
We were so excited to go, and that feeling was so
infectious.
It was Amare', his sister and their cousins' first time on a
plane.
People thought we were crazy, nuts and some said
insane.
Yes, people that thought we were crazy traveling about
in the middle of a pandemic,
In our minds there was no doubt about that time and
where we wanted to spend it.
First things first, my niece and I got on the phone and
moved heaven and earth to get us to her home.
Seven travelers to buy tickets for and we were going to
get it done.
Our plan was to get there safely and to have lots of fun.
We purchased and printed the tickets and made sure
each person had one,

The mothers, the daughters, the father, and the son.
The instructions were for each one to pack only one bag,
We weren't stopping to check in or to get in a line for a
tag.
The day of our travel we were looking like the nuns, and
the girls on Madeline,
There were seven family members walking in a straight
line.
The flight was good. The young people had fun.
We arrived in Texas safely with each and everyone.
Amare' was busy all over the place.
Every time we saw him he had a smile on his face.
We have pictures of him playing and jumping into the
pool.
Watching him play with his baby cousin was so funny
and so cool.
He played with his sister in the water and out.
He spent time with his cousins, uncles and aunt and
that's what that trip was about
It was so astonishing to see Amare' playing in the game
Between nephews and uncles and again his ankle got
sprained.
We made so many memories, and I will never forget it
the trip we took with Amare' to Texas in the middle of a
Pandemic.

# 11. Father Days

Amare' became a father when he was only 19.
Did he know what he was doing when he lied to me?
He didn't tell Ma-Ma until a few days before the baby
was born.
I felt left out, but I'll stop here with that. I won't go on.
Amare' loved his son from the day he came to the earth.
He was there to see him come into the world and loved
him with all he was worth.
Amare' always had the biggest smile when he saw his
son's face.
His heart was filled with love for his son, and it was
never out of place.
Amare' had a son and tried really hard to be a good dad.
As he tried to learn what to do. He gave it all that he
had.
I got to see Amare' play and care for his son and he tried
to stick with his son's mother but was a battle unwon.
He talked to him and fed him too.
He wasn't afraid to ask questions when he didn't know
what to do.

Amare' became a father when he was only 19.
He loved that little fellow from the moment he came on
the scene.

# 12. Graduation

We have many pictures of Amare' graduating from high
school
But I was not there, and it wasn't cool.
The school only gave out a few tickets for each person's
family.
I didn't want his Auntie to miss out since she flew in
from Georgia 'cause it was something she had to see.
We all went out to dinner after the graduation and we
sat around at the restaurant talking and reminiscing.
We were proud of what he'd accomplished, because they
closed all the schools during the pandemic, so his
graduation was such a blessing.
After graduation, he said he had plans to go to the
military.
He wasn't really sure. About his son he seemed to
worry.
The thought of leaving gave him some pause.
Was strong enough to leave him, he wasn't sure that he
was.

We celebrated with him that day and later that summer
when he turned 20.
He was very proud of himself, but he had to go work to
make some money.
His son needed shelter, clothes and shoes.
Now, he has to do what father has to do.

# 13. The Tragedy: December 7, 2022 -There's Never Gonna Be None Like You.

There's never gonna be none again. A man, a son, a
brother, a father, nephew or friend.
There's never gonna be no one like you on this earth.
None like you and that's gonna hurt.
There's never gonna be the kinda laugh, you laughed or
the kinda love you've shown that's not the worst half.
There's never gonna be a face just like mine. The one and
only never again in time.
There's never gonna be no one like you, so bright.
No one else to meet you and know what you were like.
There's never gonna be none like you again.
My grandson, your life came to such a short end.
There'll never be none like you! None like you never, not
in one million men.

# 14. Dear Amare

Dear Amare',
I will always love you more; never less.
I will always remember you and think you are the best.
Loving you is a gift I can't return to the store.
I will never love you less. I will always love you more.
Writing to you fills my heart.
Missing you tears it apart.
If I must feel and live with this pain,
I only feel it less because I know you won't feel it again.
I love you forever just like before
And don't forget, I love you more.

# 15. Why?

Why has my heart just stopped beating?  How am I still
breathing?
Why are you not here with us? Please, tell me why you
have to leave.
Why can't I stop crying? Even though I know you are
gone.
Some piece of my heart is still missing and everything in
the world seems wrong.
Amare' was our little fellow. The boy who came into our
lives so unexpectedly.
Amare' came into the world and stole my heart. And as
unexpectedly he had to  leave.
Amare' was such a funny fellow; he was smarter than
just for the streets.
Yes, he had a cunning edge but kindness that allowed
him to still be sweet.

# 16. Beyond Grief

Grief is when you experience a heart break.
Grief is when your whole body aches.
Grief is not a time when you smile.
It is a time to learn from it like you are a child.
Grief takes and shakes your soul.
Grief is a robber that makes you feel old.
Grief brings insecurity and fear and anxiety.
Grief makes me wonder if you knew what you meant to
me.

# 17. Amare's Life

Amare's Life is going to bring me joy forever.
The thought of his laughter still sparks a laugh in my
heart.
Amare's Life is going to bring me joy forever.
His smile is gonna light up the sky.
Amare's Life is going to bring me forever.
Even though his death brings me pain.
Amare's Life is going to bring me joy forever.
The memories of him singing Charlie Wilson with me is
happiness.
Amare's Life is going to bring me joy forever, but only in
my brain.

# 18. I am going to run on without you.

**18. I am going to rgo on without you.**

I am going to run on without you.
I won't like this task.
I'm going run on without you
until again we meet at last.
I am going to go on without you.
I'm going to run the good race, I'm going to hustle on in.
I am going to go on without you.
I'll settle down and I'm going to put on a grin.
I am going to go on without you.
I'm hoping I'll get the grace to walk up to you and God
let you recognize your face.
I hope he give us a chance to be present in that place
where they sing hallelujah songs. That where they
worship God all day long .
That place where days are sunny with full nights of
peace, that place where Gods promises all crying has to
ceased.

The place where a seat at the table means you'll get your fill. the place you and I will meet again if it is God's will.

# 19. The Volume of His Loss

The volume of Amare's loss is so quiet it is deafening.
The feel of his loss is all pain.
The reality of his loss my mind is still questioning. The
thought of his loss still shocks my brain.
The minutes of Amare's absence are so present. The
presence of his loss drives me insane.
The healing from his loss is slowly killing me and makes
the moment of his loss seem like yesterday.
The hurt from his loss is still heartfelt.  However, the
healing sometimes causes the pain to go away.
My faith during this loss started to fade, but I learn more
and more about my belief every day.
I've learned that the life of Amare will bring me joy
forever, and through God promises there's a chance to
see him on that great resurrection day.

# 20. They Told Us to "Right" an Impact Statement!

They said write an impact statement and tell us how you
feel,
Now that Amare's life has been taken from us? It feels
impact-fully surreal.
Write an impact statement they said. Tell us how
Amare's death changed your life.
You mean a motherless one child; a sister without her
best friend,
Another fatherless son, and who knows how that's
impacting him.
Do you mean how we won't get to hear Amare's
laughter or listen to any of his
story tales or watch as he sings a Charlie Wilson song in
my trench coat while dancing to it as well.
How we won't see if he learns a vocation or gets into
college, maybe earn a degree
Or learns from his mistakes and grows ups to be the
great man he was meant to be.

Do you mean the impact of watching his mother and
sister slowly lose their light,
Or the fear of seeing them in so much pain that they've
thought of taking their own
life.
On the day that Amare' was killed it was like walking
into the aftermath of a war
zone or a natural disaster.
His family and friends stood out in the parking lot of the
hospital screaming, trying to figure out how life would
be thereafter.
To watch as people who stood, almost over 6 ft tall
Melted away to almost nothing, feeling helpless and very
small.
Others walked in a circle while murmuring, going
around and around and around.
Others clutched their heads and hearts in pain and
others just sat down.
You asked about the impact on us because those
murderers took Amare's life,
To watch as they hunted him down, appearing to never
even think twice.
When you are a little child, they tell you monsters are
not real,
But each time we must watch those videos, I remember
that monsters are real and only thing they come to cut
down, destroy and to kill.

You ask us what's the impact on our lives of not having
Amare' around
It's like riding a bicycle with no wheel and both feet off
the ground.
It's like watching your favorite ice cream fall off the
cone
And someone hits you and knocks the rest of it out of
your hand, and you are left standing all alone.
It's like your heart has been broken into little pieces that
someone threw away,
And they try to say they are sorry, and everything will
be okay.
It's like looking forward to tomorrow, but yesterday
came too soon,
It's like waking up expecting sunshine and there isn't
even a moon.
It's like a scream that is much too quiet and a silence
that's much too loud.
It's like someone says there's a rainbow but you can't see
it behind the clouds.
It's like holding on to something because you are too
blind to see your way,
Or like standing in the sunshine but you can't see the
light of day.
It's like how in the hell did we get here without Amare'
and his murderers are still
alive.

However, I believe God when he says vengeance, oh
vengeance is mine.

# 21. This Part of My Story

This is part of my story I never thought I'd have to
write.
This is the part of my story that was never supposed to
be written by me in this life.
This part of my story where I am trying to survive
without my grandson.
This part of my life's story is a part that I would never
want written by anyone.
This is part of my story of the cruelty of man.
This is the part of my story where I believe that I've done
all I can.
This part, this part of my story where my entire family is
in pain.
This is part of my story that I don't even know how to
frame.
This is the part of my story A Once a Poem a Time,
When I am writing about my Amare' with love written
in every poem, every word and  line.